**Bigger on
the Inside**

Bigger on
the Inside
Kate Fox

smoke
STACK
BOOKS

[handwritten inscription] to Jessi wires times colder

Smokestack Books
School Farm
Nether Silton
Thirsk
North Yorkshire
YO7 2JZ
e-mail: info@smokestack-books.co.uk
www.smokestack-books.co.uk

ISBN 9781739473433

Smokestack Books
is represented by
Inpress Ltd

'Are all people like this?' the TARDIS asks when she's transported into the body of a woman called Idris in the episode 'The Doctor's Wife' written by Neil Gaiman. 'Like what?' asks Matt Smith's Doctor. 'So much bigger on the inside'.

Contents

Introduction

'Not sure about this new trend for poets writing introductions to their books,' I thought when I was one of the judges for the Forward Prizes in 2023. What happened to letting poems speak for themselves? But actually, I came to enjoy them and to appreciate the context-setting that was often being done. 'I'll have a bit of that' I thought. Especially since work focused on neurodiversity is still relatively new. And since I have a particular take.

My take is neurodivergent-affirming. That doesn't mean I'm saying autism is a super power or ADHD will help you take over the business world. But it does mean I'm resisting the deficit models that say different ways of processing the world are wrong or lesser and the bulk of research money should go into finding spurious genetic 'cures'. It also means I'm in favour of participant-led research, more support for neurodivergent young people and adults and a recognition that it is often the way the world is designed that disables us. It means I recognise that people with higher support needs such as those with learning disabilities, or who are non-verbal, have a different experience from those of us with lower support needs. Their strengths are often under-recognised, as are our challenges. It means that people who are additionally marginalised by ethnicity, class, sexuality, physical disability find it even harder to find diagnosis and support.

Not that I think poetry is the solution. But I do think giving a different perspective can help move some of the dials that are finally shifting.

This collection is a mixture of spoken word pieces and poems. The distinction is a whole other introduction – but basically I do find a difference between writing primarily for performance and primarily for the page. Sometimes they overlap. I write in lots of different registers and voices and finally being okay with that is part of my 'unmasking' more as a neurodivergent writer.

'Bigger on the Inside' is a spoken word show I started developing in 2017 after my Autism diagnosis. The pandemic has delayed its full outing – but I'm glad, because in that time many more young people and adults have become aware of their neurodivergent identity and are looking for positive representations of it.

The Doctor in the sci fi series *Doctor Who* has long been recognised by neurodivergent people as 'one of us' – a role model of thinking and feeling differently, fighting for truth and fairness and liking Jelly Babies. In this collection are also some of the pieces from a show I began developing in 2011 called 'A Portrait of the Autist as a Young Woman'. It was a bit ahead of where both myself and audiences were at the time, but in taking it to a conference I discovered the theory of 'Monotropism' developed by Wenn Lawson and Dinah Murray, among others and realised that the idea of having either highly focused or highly scattered attention defined by my life as a writer – and as a person. It's wonderful that the theory is now receiving wider recognition – and there is a tribute in the show to autistic elder Dinah Murray who I was lucky enough to get to know a bit before she died in 2021.

Several of the poems in the show and in the rest of this collection take their titles from *Doctor Who* episodes. The final section, which looks to the future, explores a universe in which a neurodivergent-affirming world becomes possible thanks to a surprising intervention by trees. It's a kind of *Doctor Who* episode in poetic form, or rather, the poetic equivalent of the spin-off series *Torchwood*.

I was inspired by Dr Nick Walker's idea of 'Neuroqueering' – which basically means subverting the ways of being and thinking and imagining that we see as normal and natural. Since this moves beyond focusing just on biological differences to recognise how much our ways of being are influenced by our gender, ethnicity, class and sexuality, I think it holds huge potential as a set of practices for re-imagining a more diversity-friendly ecology in all senses. The penultimate poem of the collection 'The Lie of the Land' ends with words from some

Doctor Who speeches which have always already galvanised a 'Neuroqueer imagination' to envision a fairer, kinder world. Just as other figures I write about did – including Lorna Wing, who came up with the Autism Spectrum, Dinah Murray, and the Brontes (who made a surprise appearance in my poems and in this section but very insistently claimed their place).

Kate Fox, 2024

Bigger on the Inside

The world in an atom
full of space and charge.
It's not that those before us lied,
they just could not see
we were bigger on the inside.
The thoughts and feelings
you share and hide
make you bigger on the inside.

We only see five per cent of the universe
the rest is dark matter and energy,
the void between the trapeze
and the gaze fixed
on movement's blur.
An absence of something can be a guide
to what is bigger on the inside.
Some of us froze when we tried
to forget we too
were bigger on the inside

White space speaks
while the fonts stay quiet.
I called the counselling group women
midwives of silence
because they let words
hang in the air.
The gap between what is sent
and what's replied,
what is stated, what's implied.
Language is bigger on the inside.

We only see five per cent of the universe
 the rest is dark matter and energy.
An absence can show only
what we have to hide
under the masks
we are all bigger on the inside.
Mourning expands us
to absorb those who died,
making us bigger on the inside.

A marriage is an enclave
with soft borders
whose language is dying out
from the day it is learned.
I broke the contract but tried
to know how couples
become bigger on the inside.
With every category you elide
you grow bigger on the inside.

You absorb people like sunlight,
be careful not to burn,
even a day can tire you out.
Keep them at a safe distance
though as you warm your hands
they may think
you are warding them off.
Measuring visible behaviours
long denied
the ways we are bigger on the inside

A stage is where the distance between performer
and audience
and each full seat in the auditorium
is filled with something
invisible and weightless
and powerful as electrons colliding.
The stories we tell and hear
will abide
to make us bigger on the inside.

Once Upon a Time Part I

- Once upon a time there was a girl called K who didn't like egg whites or cheese or tomatoes or crumpets, who could recite the capitals of European countries when she was two and didn't seem to hear lots of things that were said to her. This is true.

- When she was seven she started making a list of all the words and their meanings, but then she found out that a man called Samuel Johnson had that idea some timé ago, so she was able to stop.

- Birthday cards and Christmas cards said 'With Love from Mum and Dad', but K was not sure what this word meant. They didn't give her hugs or many kind words but they did make sure she had enough to eat and clothes to wear and books to read. The thing her Dad said most often was that he never lied.

- K left home when she was sixteen when she found out about some lies her parents had told. Her father told everybody that she was a liar. It turned out that he wasn't her father, so he had lied. This helped her realise that he was lying about her lying, which could have been confusing if she still believed that he only told the truth. Now she wasn't sure about the word 'Dad' or 'Love', or even the word 'Lying'. This is true. Her Mum and Dad said it wasn't up to them to make sure she had enough to eat and clothes to wear and books to read anymore, and signed the letter 'Love'.

- All truth is relative, but not all relatives are the truth.

- After that K found it even more difficult to say words that didn't fit the pictures in her brain, or the pictures that she thought might be in other people's brains. She didn't say parts of her body out loud very much. Not because she was prudish, but because it didn't feel like the parts and the words matched.

- She couldn't connect photographs to her memories of the things they photographed, or metaphors to her memories of what they were compared to. She called photographs and metaphors lies, which seemed very strange to people who felt their truth, or didn't feel their truth but didn't notice or care.

- When she talked about her first boyfriend who had been sent to prison, she called him 'The caged friend overseas who I was intimately interacting with'. Luckily, to her university friends, compared to sentences about Postmodernism or Post-canonical fiction, this seemed perfectly understandable.

- When K met her real father, he didn't mind that it took her a thousand words and some pictures and similes to say a simple word like 'family'. This made her feel like they were family.

- Sixty days later when he died, K couldn't feel the feelings she didn't have words for, or say the words for those feelings she wasn't quite able to feel. She did suspect that the feeling of all those unfelt feelings and unsaid words was like carrying an unexploded bomb.

- Then a stepmother came into the story. Not a wicked step-mother, but one who had a special wisdom about how sometimes people are family, even if they don't fit the rules about who is supposed to be in a family. She said sentences like 'I love you' and 'This is home' and these words felt true in K's brain and heart but she couldn't make words that said them back, even though she knew that was what her stepmother wanted.

2017

- Jodie Whittaker, from Huddersfield in West Yorkshire, becomes *Doctor Who*'s first female Doctor.

- I am in the process of completing my PhD in stand-up comedy and therefore becoming a doctor. Not 'Oops my pancreas hurts' sort of doctor. After being told there was a lack of expertise around the diagnosis of women in my area I went privately to the University of Kent's Tizard Centre for the autism diagnosis I had been wondering about for over a decade.

- In 2017 there are still said to be two men to every one woman who are autistic – though a few years earlier it had supposedly been ten men to every woman.

The Girl Who Waited

I

A woman from Huddersfield
sets a course for the stars

one of my neurokin says
he didn't know he wasn't supposed

to go from a Newcastle comp
to being a musician,

the unlikelihood
hadn't been wired in.

Another never fitted
with gangs on the council estate.

Prison or addiction
his likely fate,

he wanted to take photographs,
found a darkroom at eleven,

developed negatives in silver nitrate.
Playground bullies asked me

'Who do you think you are?'
and the freedom lay in having no idea.

If you don't know how to play the game you're in
 or even that you're in one

you're free to find another way to win,
or at least, become a magnet,

or iron filings, attracted to the forces
which are not boring or baffling.

II

Of course I could have become Prime Minister
or a Northern newsreader or stand-up poet

on Radio Four, while not understanding
how to snog someone at a club,

keep a plant or human alive,
imagine serving drinks in a pub.

Of course it looks like delusion or arrogance
if you sing your own song, dance your own dance

as you dodge the symbolic violence
which demands your complicity

compels your silence:
not spongily absorbing

social rules becomes accidental
partial inoculation

against the mental colonisation
of neo liberalization

(With sentences like that as my tool can't think why
I wasn't more popular at my Bradford secondary school.)

My diagnosis was missed cos for girls in the late eighties,
like a template for a 'normal' person,

it didn't exist; there were gaps:
routes for which everyone else had maps

Scarce Attention

I last saw Dinah
catapulted across the pewter mirror
of Dalgety Bay in a pair of coconut shells,

her son told us to think of her
when we saw rainbows,
and I do.

Attention is finite,
focused as a torch beam,
diffuse as a fountain.

*At any one moment the amount of attention available to a conscious
individual is limited. The limited availability of attention plays a
fundamental role in everyday life*

'Cut a flower it does not bleed
the sap withdraws
but the seed flowers again.'

Dinah recites her childhood poem
in the improvised sickroom
where she sits yellow and dying

while her old friend Sue makes lentil soup for visitors
and I fiddle with the Voice Memo settings on my iPhone
with more urgency than usual

*Monotropic focus will mean both tending to perform the task well
and tending to lose awareness of information relevant to all other
tasks.*

Things I have thought could be added to the diagnostic criteria
for autism:
Collecting mushrooms.
Having a fantasy of moving to a commune or island in Scotland,
Liking octopuses and/or me.

Dinah knows she is lichen,
that there are more bacteria in her gut
than stars in the galaxy, that we are all processes.

*As Jordan observed, the individual with autism tends to be 'a
phenomenologist, trying to learn from what is seen, heard, felt, smelt,
rather than from what can be implied or inferred from these
sensations.'*

Her Doctor Who costume would be a hoodie,
an anorak and walking boots

an Opinel fungi knife tucked in an inside pocket,
along with a tangled handful of *Hyndum Repandum*,
Grifola frondosa and *Agaricus bisporus*.

But above all, *Monotropa uniflora*,
the mushroom sharing her theory's name,
its mycelium strands connecting those of us
who thrive when we can focus on

ONE THING AT A TIME

*Individuals on the autism spectrum tend to be either passionately
interested or not interested at all.*

Feeling intensely the joy of connecting,
the pain of being stuck in a glass house
confused by sudden shake-ups outside our tunnels of attention.

Dinah campaigned for computers and assistive tech
so autistic people in care could communicate
their needs (and interests).

I forgot to turn my wi-fi signal off
so some parts of the interview I record
end up in slurred robot voice

Repeated failure to meet their own and other people's expectations
may lead to dread, a dominant emotion for many people with autism

I hope I've captured the most important parts:
how she's dying happy because she lived her mission
for a fairer world

and now more people
are pushing that boulder up the hill.
Remember your enemy's interests

overlap with yours.
You just have to keep on planting the seeds.
Love your neighbour, change their mind

We think the root of the social problems sometimes regarded as core
in autism is probably attentional

Peter Capaldi's Doctor saying
'Above all be kind, just kind'
in my head

Badges on scarves
still carry her phrases; 'Weird Pride',
'Productive Irritant'

that have lasted from her time
on her UNIT equivalent:
the National Autistic Taskforce.

*In a social world in which rules were simple, clear and invariant,
monotropism might not be a hindrance*

She fought for 'Autistic liberation'
even before realising it was her own,
knew no one group gains freedom alone.

As she said, where you focus your force
is not usually
a medical matter

but underpins the stuff
that distinguishes one human
from another.

*The reward for neurotypical people for the effort of tuning in to the
interests and emotional states of monotropic individuals may be
equally intense.*

Networks of stars
constellations of fungi,
rhizomes of humans

diffuse perspectives ways of being
held in harmony

held in tension.
revealed as Dinah compelled us
to pay deeper attention

Attention Tunnel

Don't pull me out
of the attention tunnel
where time collapses
and scattered thoughts funnel.
There's a toll to pay to enter here
but once I'm in
money, socks and post disappear

Don't pull me out of the attention tunnel,
it's nothing personal about not liking you
or the things you're inviting me to do
though you're not currently as interesting
as the things in there
that much is true.

Don't pull me out
of the attention tunnel:
it's like wrenching a barnacle from a rock;
sticky residue will be left behind;
I'll only retain half my mind

It's like interrupting any performer in their flow.
Let's hope no-one would go

to Ronnie O'Sullivan cueing up
a championship shot:
'Oi, Ronnie, do you want to see this
lovely new cardigan I just got?'

or to Simone Biles
in quadruple axel poise,
'Hey Simone, what do you think of neo liberal capital
globalisation,
and also, boys?'

or to David Tennant at the RSC,
about to Hamletly ask
'To be or not to be?'
'David, Daaaavid, it's time for your tea!'

Don't pull me out of the attention tunnel
when I'm a laser beam that can focus and think,
my mind and body for once in sync,
the pain of awareness pulling back
like a turtle's neck while it's retracting

Don't pull us out of the tunnel of –
what? I forgot.
Because your attention is –
distracting.

1963

- The first *Doctor Who* episode 'An Unearthly Child' is broadcast on 23rd November. The show was conceived by the BBC as an educational series for children.

- Empowered by the Mental Health Act, the 'Society for Autistic Children' is started by a group of progressive psychologists and parents, whose children had previously officially been classed as 'idiots', 'imbeciles' and 'ineducable'. The professionals include the psychiatrist Lorna Wing. She begins the first statistical study of autism which goes on to recognise that what was then 'Classic Autism' with learning disabilities and what she came to name 'Asperger's' after Austrian psychiatrist Hans Aspergers* studies, are part of what she called 'The autistic spectrum'.

- I am minus twelve years old. My mum is fourteen and realising that the pleasure of filing and typing and putting things out of place into the right place means she should do a secretarial course in Leeds when she leaves school the following year.

On the Wing

Lorna Wing,
Sparrow bright eyes
medical student,
who specialised:
then psychiatrist,
Mother to Susie
and the first to realise

her non-verbal daughter,
and many more of us
including her fellow grey, grey, grey feathered
psychiatrists,
who loved to flock together and systemise

would be recognised
if we became something psychiatry
could categorise
because someone whose struggles are seen,
can have their differences nurtured,
become someone who flies.

Her daughter and thousands of others
were written off officially
as 'idiots', 'ineducable', 'imbeciles'.
So she helped develop a taxonomy,
to ornithologise
describing the 'active but odd',
'passive', 'aloof' and 'rigid' types
they spotted alongside the ones
with 'learning difficulties'.

Here was the Autistic Spectrum
she named,
but as so often, a linear label,
came to disguise
the phenomenon it tries
to describe. Stuck in a hide,
binoculars fixed,
the psychiatrists began to pathologise
the children Lorna Wing
had been trying to personalise,
those she had begun to recognise
as not 'psychotic' or 'stuck in their own worlds'
but disabled by sensory overwhelm.

These rare species,
their feeding, mating,
self-soothing, sensory seeking
and avoiding, migrating (or not) behaviours
ticked off.
They went official with their
lists and pictures,
in a way that came to dehumanise
people now seen as 'robotic' –
for the differences
in the ways they socialise

though Lorna knew she was one of the birds
not just one of the twitchers
'Nature never draws a line
without smudging it' she said,
and 'autistic traits
help success in the sciences and the arts',
something researchers are only just now
beginning to analyse.

But her holistic knowing
was broken down into parts
for the diagnostic manuals.
Those inadvertent lies
get told when behaviours
are taken for being.
Losing Lorna's emphasis on *dimensions*
of autistic experience
which allowed for new seeing
of women, people of colour,
anyone other than white guys.

I picture her in the diagnostic centre
that bears her name,
just a few years before dementia clouded
her sharp brain. Owl-wise.
Telling me she'd let a fox
out of the conservatory
just before I came.
Being the first person to consider
I might be more comfortable
without the fluorescent light.
Her ability to imagine
a better future for us
still in flight.

1975

- Tom Baker's first season as the Doctor continues with one of the most iconic episodes 'Genesis of the Daleks' in which their creator Davros first appears and the Doctor makes his famous 'Have I the Right?' speech when he has the chance to prevent the creation of the Daleks if he touches two wires together.

- Autistic children are now characterised as 'robotic' with no interior lives by psychologists, having been seen, up until the 1960s, as 'psychotic' and with an excess of imagination.

- Ten days after the serial 'Revenge of the Cybermen' ends, me and my twin brother are born.

We Are (Definitely) Not Daleks

Fluorescent lights,
restless nights.
Social cues,
uncomfy shoes
Just Tolerate Just Tolerate

Got distracted,
didn't hear,
just wanted things
to be clear.
Need for detail
and accuracy
making others think that we
Interrogate Interrogate

Relationships
we've craved or feared,
online dating
is just weird,
pressure to conform
or breed
hyper or hypo sexual need
Let's mask our fate
Mask our Fate

Supermarkets
and unexpected guests that hurt,
the prickly label
in that shirt
traumatic drill,
sudden bill,
overload not under-use
of will
Aggravate
Aggravate

The times we tried
but didn't fit,
were bamboozled,
or gaslit,
just want our tribe
accepted more
not studied by boffins
to find a cure
Exterminate Exterminate

Protection's not a metal case
it's empathy
that won't erase
the ways we differ on the inside,
here's this symbol
of Autistic Pride
It's lemniscate
It's lemniscate

People who don't mean
what they say,
want you doing things
the 'normal' way,
Don't interrupt or complicate
nor repeat or hesitate
Don't Deviate
Don't Deviate

We're not one tribe
but recognise
a walk, a wince,
a flick of eyes,
liberation for one
liberation for all
hear this as a collective call
Co-operate
Co-operate

Life's hard too
for dominant neurotypes,
normality is not worth
the hype,
on diversity, the tide is turning
unity's needed
cos the world is burning
Love not Hate
Love not Hate

One of the Meltdowns I Never Had

Arrgh, tomatoes!
Crumpets with their little holes.
My tongue is unhappy.
Hoovers so loud
inside my brain
they might whoosh me up.
Lifts zooming. How do I hold on?
Escalators. Might fall in,
everything mov-
itchy, itchy, it's all itchy!
Wool, labels, tights,
itchy, moving world,
bright, bright lights.
Smoke! Cough!
What did they say?
'Say pardon not what'.
but what?
What? Arrgh!
Not the soggy Weetabix
sick feeling in my mouth
coldjellysalt spam
itchy, itchy, moving, moving
arrrggggghhhhh.

What I actually express is this:

😐

1989

* *Doctor Who*'s viewing figures are steadily declining and the controller of the BBC Michael Grade had long had it in his sights to cancel. After a final season with Sylvester McCoy as the Doctor and Sophie Aldred as his companion Ace, it bows out with the Doctor's words: 'There are worlds out there where the sky is burning. And the sea's asleep, and the rivers dream. People made of smoke, and cities made of song. Somewhere there's danger. Somewhere there's injustice. Somewhere else, the tea's getting cold. Come on, Ace – we've got work to do!'

* The diagnostic test, the A-DOS, is made available to psychologists and psychiatrists, allowing a massive increase in the diagnosis of Aspergers and Autism. The film *Rain Man* is released with Dustin Hoffman's portrayal of an autistic mathematical savant helping his card shark brother played by Tom Cruise, becoming many people's definitive idea of adult autism.

* Meanwhile, as a fourteen-year-old at a comprehensive school in Bradford, my own permission to be eccentric is being cancelled. I take solace in books and more books. Oh – also, with the fall of the Berlin Wall and collapse of Communism, neo liberal capitalism gets under way in the US and UK. Watch out if you're not productive enough for growth capitalism!

Silence in the Library

I was a library kid,
among the dusty shelves I hid

and browsed, discovered different worlds,
from *Sweet Valley High* to *What Katy Did.*

Adult conversations with the librarian,
learning how to be contrarian

reading the *Mail,* the *Guardian,*
*Hansar*d and Private Eye

inside at break times, warm and dry,
loosening my strangulating school tie.

The relief and quiet of carpeted floors
escaping echoey corridors
away from dinner-ladies, bullies and bores.

Once and always a library kid
dreaming of islands or going off-grid

we all need sanctuaries
to be gently with others, or alone,

in your room,
your car, a beach, your phone

or deep safe inside yourselves
still miles and miles of library shelves.

Stim

Words with a beat
bind your voice and your feet.

Poetry with a rhyme,
connects your ears up with time.

Words with a rhythm
link your mind to your heart.

A verse and a stanza
merge the whole and the part.

Living images
fuse your speech and your sight.

Your hand
and your brain work as one when you write.

Emotion and idea blend to heal your soul. Music can make
what's separate feel whole.

Similes knit together
like your bones after a break.

you see your metaphorical reflection in an imaginary lake.
Poems set up expectations and meet them in a line

and sometimes they don't.

Another Meltdown I Didn't Have
(while radio newsreader for a cool radio
station in Manchester in 2001)

Techno, techno, techno, banging,
strobing lights, strobing,
people's limbs flailing like windmills.
Avoid! Their mouths like dark tunnels. Avoid!
The pixellated people,
my brain fuzzy from that one Cinzano Bianco I had.
'Just one' they said
like always, now bzzzzzzz.
Everything buzzing. Outside. I could get away,
flee away. Airrrrrr!
The bouncer points at a man by the taxi rank.
'Taxiiiii, taxiiii' but he laughs. He's not a taxi man.
I will fight this, go back to the bouncers and complain.
'That was dangerous, he wasn't a taxi driver,
you pointed me to a random man!'
Their shiny jackets, their shiny eyes,
a blank wall, their lies, lies!
Coming closer, stepping towards me.

My face does this

😐

My body does this

🙅

and I'm on the ground,
then in the hospital,
only bruised,
then back on air next morning

reading the news
and talking to the presenter
about what went on.
Later the officer taking my statement
said he heard me on his drive to work,
thought 'That's the CCTV gone',
though actually it wasn't expunged.
Later, I saw it in an interview room,
a trio of blurred black and white figures
until one of them – me – lunged.

2005

- Doctor Who returns with Russell T Davies as show runner, Christopher Ecclestone as the Doctor and Billie Piper as his companion, Rose Tyler.

- Autistic activists have been connecting online across the world since the mid-nineties, on listservs. Alex Plank's 'Wrong Planet' has thousands of forum users. Autreat in the US and Autscape in the UK have just begun, as annual retreats for autistic people to meet in the real world and share knowledge outside the narratives of medical professional and parents.

- I have been working as a radio journalist and newsreader and started performing at, and running poetry events. I've also done a counselling course at college as part of my ongoing quest to understand the baffling species known as humans – and, in common with one of my counselling teachers, am just starting to tentatively connect with the few available narratives by autistic adults as possibly explaining a few things. Here is what I did: I went on counselling courses and had counselling to help me learn the rules of people. I picked a counsellor who had also been on counselling courses and had counselling to help him learn the rules of people. We both became much better at discovering the thoughts and feelings of others from what their bodies and faces and words showed, and in return showing our thoughts and feelings to other people using our faces and bodies and words. But there was still another language that other people spoke that neither of us knew, and we couldn't get anybody to tell us why we couldn't hear it, though we looked for the answer in thousands of books and thousands of conversations with people who spoke it. Then we discovered that a people who were called Autistic also didn't hear this language and we felt like we had found our kin, but being accepted as part of the kin required tests and we had become too good at the other languages to manage to fail them.

How Do You Know?

You stare at coins in a loud place,
failing to connect them with numbers,
look again at the magic trick
on a screen,
the one where two people lean forward
at exactly the same time
to kiss each other
without a word passing between them.
How did they know?
How did they know?
In books, those must be the paragraphs
they print in invisible ink.
Did you notice they were pretending?
No.
Did you notice she was angry?
No.
How did you know?
When their mouths have stopped
shaping sounds across the wires,
how do you know?
You're a flooded car engine
waiting to clear,
a computer crashing
when too many programs
are open at once.
But in quiet places
you calculate risks and outcomes
quick and accurate as a loss adjuster,
pretend like everyone else
that repetition is the same as prediction,
sense something like heat that rises

from people when they look at you.
Is it what they'll tell you it is?
How do they know?
How do you know?

Autistic Joy

Sparkly things
Octopuses
Sparkly octopuses
Correcting someone who thinks the plural of octopuses
is octopi
Doing it in a poem
Autistic Joy, an instant high
Dungarees with dogs on
Contagious excitement
about the server in Pret's guinea pig dress!
And how it has pockets!
And her guinea pigs will also recognise on it pictures
of their own food-bits of cucumber and apple!
A retro flavour of Snapple
An info dump about my Sebo vacuum cleaner,
bought after extensive joyous research
Electric blue stained glass with light slanting through
in a furniture polish-scented church
A right rhyme
at the right time
and the unchimeability of orange
Spotting patterns on your bedspread,
in their conversation,
in the icing on a Chelsea bun
A perfect pun –
like my Buddhist friend
who said the new Covid strain
would be called Om om omicron...
The right silver of sea
combined with the right angle of sun
Bonding over 'ha ha ha,
neurotypical people asking 'How are you?'
and giving them an honest answer'

Becoming spinner, tapper, conductor, rhythm,
dancer
Your favourite brand of same food
back on the shelf
A new amazing fact
about your favourite act
A notebook or under-eye perfectly lined
The endless sparks and connections of your own mind
Here, put that in your pipe
make it officially diagnostic
no one does joy like a joyful autistic.

Once Upon a Time Part II

- In a group of people who met in a cosy room near the sea to discover truths about who they were, K eventually began to feel safe enough to feel feelings, and then to fit words to the feelings, and in this way K realised that many of the words that other people used for feelings weren't a lie after all.

- K spent some time with a man who she could only lose, maybe so that she could finally explode her unexploded bomb and find some words for the feelings she hadn't known how to feel and the words she hadn't known how to say.

- Imagine a caption over a picture of bomb exploding that says 'Lots of Poems'.

- On a trip to Amsterdam, K stayed with the family of a woman she'd met on a writing course and used their warm home as a base while she explored the streets and canals, the Van Gogh museum and Anne Frank's house. She heard the Dutch word *gezellig*. She read that it isn't translatable into English, but covers cosy cafes, candlelit warmth, the feeling of meeting a friend after a long time and a sense of belonging.

- K *felt* like she knew just what this meant.

- It was the feeling at her group, in dim light in a warm living room, talking truths with her friend at a seaside cafe, curling up on the settee with the affectionate dog she was dogsitting, putting up the Christmas tree at her step mother's house for the 17th year in a row...

- She began to feel *gezellig* feelings all the time...

- Then she met a man who seemed unlikely to get lost. He had lots of very accurate words for feelings because he was a good writer, but also, he didn't mind not having words for some feelings and was good at helping their bodies and hearts speak very loudly.

- He said being with K felt familiar, felt like the end of a nostalgia for something he had never known. He said it was like the Welsh phrase *brith gof,* which doesn't have an equivalent in English but is sometimes translated as 'faint recollection' or 'speckled memory'.

- With him, K felt *gezellig* nearly all the time.

- *Gezellig* plus *brith gof* = Love.

- His favourite film was *Amelie*, a French film about a childlike French woman who tries to help people but needs to look after herself so she can find love. He said K was Amelie and he was Amelie and they watched the film together. The good thing was that he was also himself and she was also herself. More feelings came and now many of them had names, K didn't ask as many questions about words.

- Well most of the time... He gave K an engagement ring. Straight away she asked 'What does engagement mean?' 'What do people do in engagement?', because 'engagement' wasn't a well enough explained word, just by itself.

- And now, when her stepmum said 'I love you', she knew exactly what she meant when she said it back. And she doesn't mind when K uses a thousand words, a few similes and some pictures to say a not very simple word like 'family'.

- K even has some of her wedding photographs up, along with her signed photograph of David Tennant and Billie Piper.

- These are the sort of stories that can happen to anybody, whether or not the word 'autism' is in their story.

- K was a poet at a conference where nurses were talking about care and compassion by attending to the humanity of the patient with all of themselves and she thought that really they were talking about love. She heard performers talking about what it's like when they're accepted by an audience and they accept an audience's responses and thought that really they were talking about love and when scientists talk about the attention they're paying to the way that a parent and baby are sharing their attention, she thought that really they're talking about love...

- Not The End.

2015

- Steve Silberman's influential book *Neurotribes*, which started as an article about something called 'Silicon Valley Syndrome' among computer geeks in California, and explores the development of conflicting ideas of autism, is published.

- Although I made a show which explored whether I might get a diagnosis of autism with a title which seemed to pre-empt a conclusion: 'Portrait of the Autist as A Young Woman' I never fully toured it and am now doing my PhD on Northernness and comedy. Even after my diagnosis, the journey to embodying my neurodivergent identity will be an ongoing process.

- While I am living a 'hybrid' identity as sort of possibly autistic, discovering what a 'masked' or 'camouflaged' autistic identity might be, companion Clara Oswald (Jenna Coleman) and Peter Capaldi's Doctor threatened all of time and space by becoming a prophesied 'Hybrid' – though hybridity is part of the show (the TARDIS has mixed with Rose Tyler and River Song while the Metacrisis Doctor and Donna Noble shared DNA).

Turn Left

I'm not saying I make bad relationship decisions
but when I was sixteen
I lost my virginity
to a 46-year-old gunrunner
my choices guided by a mixture of *Jane Eyre*
and *Doctor Who*
although of course, the latter is not true:

before it returned in 2005,
there was no sex in the Whoniverse,
despite Peri's low-cut tops For The Dads.
So, what was worse,
I had to go by my undeveloped internal compass,
Cosmo's advice page,
social norms in the era of the Spice Girls and Jimmy Saville
and make do.

At least they were mostly nice men
after the unfortunate sociopathic start,
enjoying – some – of my still quite masked quirks
and kind to my heart.
But 2005's return of Who
meant nothing less than
crying on a Norwegian beach
as the love of my life fades to a hologram
while finally declaring his feelings,
or someone who'd guard my tomb for two thousand years
like Rory did for Amy Pond
as the Last Centurion,
(who said trauma bond?)
would do.

My marriage didn't survive
me exploring my more autistic me
though discovering who you actually are
when you're undiagnosed neurodivergent
can be a long and difficult journey

and I'm no longer the manic pixie dream girls
Clara and Amy of the Steven Moffatt era,
more like Saga from *The Bridge* –
or, actually, *Vera.*

And now my relationship rules
come from attachment and trauma experts on Instagram
noticing red flags and boundaries
expressing who I really am

so if I saw an ad
for: *A gender-fluid, two thousand-year-old, neurodivergent*
digital nomad,
hashtag vanlife,
seeking a companion for adventure, fun, travel,
planet-saving and occasional Netflix and chill,
experience in screaming and running an advantage,
triggering experiences and memory-wiping
a high possibility
have I learned my lesson,
would I feel bereft
if I broke the pattern
and swiped left?

Mask

Here is a girl standing alone in the middle of a white aircraft-
hanger who needs somebody to take her hand;
here is a girl joyously kicking up brown leaves.

People mostly see only one of these.
Here is a girl wearing a badly-fitting clown mask
plastic mouth rim digging into her top lip

and a girl in a lacy blue body suit
which raises a red rash on her tummy.

Here is a girl who can make a room full of strangers
come to hug her like their own.

Here is a girl who doesn't quite recognise herself,
though there are always plenty of photos.

Here is a girl who became a woman,
who can see behind masks and round corners
and hear the gaps between words and things
where light pours like falling water.

Here is a woman who knows
she can travel as fast as rewind
to where the girl stands alone
in a hanger filled with the sound
of arrivals and departures.

Here is a woman who knows
it will never be too late to stand alongside
the girl in the hanger,
take hold of her hand and squeeze.

A Meltdown I Didn't Have in a Buddhist Temple

Crowds of people surged towards the overflow exit,
a canvas door tied with ropes.
Inside I am screaming 'Get away from the loud,
moving people'
which is not as Buddhist as 'Be compassionate
to all sentient beings'
but thanks to a year of meditation
I did listen to my inner voice,
instinctively moved to the edge of the tent,
crouched down, made myself small,
let my heartbeat slow,
and after waiting and waiting for the bottleneck to go,
asked a nearby monk if there was another way out.
With no energy for preamble or euphemism
I said 'I'm autistic, I can't be in here anymore'.
He pointed across the main temple building;
'Over there's the handicapped door'.
I didn't say, 'Is it the seventies?' or
'is your door unwell?',
just made a break, like a meerkat breaching cover,
but even after crossing the thankfully empty plains,
with flashes of gold, statues, flowers,
there were still queues of people
and I didn't know if the fire door was as alarmed as me.
Then I saw a friendly face from my local centre,
no spare spoons to explain, said
'I really need to get out of here,
someone pointed me to the 'handicapped' exit
but I don't know if I can get through it'.
she swung into action, put her red steward's sash across her chest,
like a superhero cape,
held out her hand, which I gripped tightly,
fully accepting the rescue,

led me past the people, out, out into the air,
where my brain-body relaxed in relief at being out of there,
as she apologised to a nun-steward, heading off any criticism
for breaking the rules
'She has a hidden   , she has an invisible   '
And for different reasons
I also lacked words
to fill in the gaps.

Once Upon a Time Part III

- K has discovered how to write poetry in the style of contemporary British poets circa the early twenty first century, and Buddhist meditation.

- The Poets often say things like 'Poetry allows you to say what cannot be said.

- By now she has learned words like 'Alexithymia' – which means a difficulty processing and recognising your own feelings.

The Hug

The hug had been looking for the likes of us;
frustrating itself with the trampoline bounce of a puffa jacket
off a leather sleeve,
a wing flap of hand across back,
a door check of head over shoulder
in the rounds of house party goodbyes.

It found us – who had exchanged only a few words –
it found us with the shock of prayers in a foreign church
when you've just gone in to look at the ceiling.

It kept us for the whole length of a song,
orange lights playing in our heads,
for an airport travelator of still movement,
for a microwave defrosting lasagne, quietly pulsing.

It ignored the onlooker who said
'I'm starting to get uncomfortable now',
the one who clung on to our sides,
for an awkward turn of the carousel
before falling back laughing.

It held us while we kept rowing towards the other side of the
river, dragonflies hovering above our wake,
a gull wheeling in a slow arc toward the lighthouse.

Held us, while the sonographer's wand
criss-crossed a stomach,
and the diver's torch lit fronds whose waving
brings everything they need to nourish them.

It only sighed and breathed,
until one of us murmured
'Everybody else lets go too soon'.

Shutdown

Talking about actual things became
like when 'No internet connection' keeps coming up
and also your laptop is crackling and spattering
like angry bacon

and avoiding a pavement crack
because the pavement crack might confirm
its love and attraction for others
and I'd only reached NVQ level in Buddhist non-attachment

and thus might melt like a snowman
leaving only a wrinkled carrot,
it being several weeks more until I'd be able
to stay upright at such reality

and several months more until due
to be initiated in the wrathful compassion
of *Vajrayogini* who apparently can say 'Fuck you'
with great kindness

which would possibly resonate in your
own crackling laptop, ever prone to sudden shutdowns,
becoming mushroom cloud or white light
or the concrete lip round the seventh floor
of a brutalist car park.

Thus, to avoid the melting etc,
we have negotiated without speaking
something that feels like a Youtube video
of people walking gingerly across a glass bridge

with only this poem, at my end, and the other ones
now emerging as if from a steam room into an empty spa
where a pool waits, still as a portrait,
for a swimmer or the cover of night.

Dissociation

Like a tortoise head retracting under threat,
what you called your feelings for me
might stop for two days, two weeks, two months,
governed by some twinning internal clock.

I lived for the flood back,
realised this might not be so much a problem
for you as a rhythm, but nonetheless began to mirror
the cut-offs, the returns

perhaps searching for a solution internally
I could present back to you like an owl
with a digested mouse pellet.
Instead, found a balm to earlier wounds

a Buddhist monk saying 'Your feelings do not matter',
training in *compassion*, a sure and steady flow
offered to everyone without exception
including myself. Internally now; a constant nightlight glow.

Annoyingly Magical

Sometimes I managed a day on my own,
that felt briefly magical as ordinary ones
with you. Particularly vexing

after I understood our minds,
not external others,
produce feelings.
What mechanism was this?

It wasn't a yellow flowers get yellower,
blue walls get bluer post-trip type feeling
or sheer joy at your presence thing.

It worked even watching people limp,
scoot, straggle on a grey day in South Shields,
on a Christmas bingo afternoon

in a Northern club with father and son
Elvis and Johnny Cash,
Donna's crucifix, Jade's hat.

They became a Stanley Spencer,
or Klimt's Kiss which you'd cried before,
both of us standing in different awe.

You explained to others how
I was good at things you weren't
and vice versa.

Sometimes you'd ask me to transmute
your words. The relief for me was
you'd already returned mine to my body

so I didn't have to say it was as if
our different minds
were interlocking jigsaw pieces

clicking so a door precision engineered
by a medieval craftsperson
who didn't have access to nails or B&Q,

could open releasing golden light,
a conga, a forest and everything,
everything else became a gallery or a dream.

Finding the Object of Negation

The sun insistent behind the monk's ear,
red traceries of vein visible.
Another place the self
is not to be found;
he has just asked us to look for it.

It is not in the muffled trombone trills
elicited by last night's lentil dal
(which contained also clouds, garlic, patience, turmeric,
a comet and the Buddhas of the ten directions).

It is not in the left buttock which, in any case,
went numb during the Liberating Prayer,
or in the shocked expression
when the warden said the lines
were, in fact, yellow

or in the stream of thoughts
which could be rendered something like,
'Hedges like mountains... my neighbour's angry eyes
...shears are big scissors'

Which led into a memory
of the Christmas he pulled the tree down.

It is not in the temporal fusiform gyrus (take that on faith),
or the stray quote floating onto an internal screen
in Times New Roman about 'An experiencer
experiencing themselves as the experienced',
nor in our fungal left toenail.

It goes without saying that it is not
in the thumb and forefinger
holding the pen, the motor impulse to move the hand,
the synapses firing as it does,
or the retinas scanning emergent syllables.

Not in the neurological region calling up
some line about stars, a wood panelled room,
a bear pacing a closet, a reflecting moon
at the end of a pointing finger,
a sky darkening to purple which widens beyond
its edges to a panorama while
in the background, a very, very faint whistle.

2023

'With sufficient engagement in neuroqueer practice, anyone can liberate themselves from the strictures of normativity. The already neurodivergent can reconnect with, and cultivate previously suppressed or undeveloped capacities, in order to more fully manifest their potentials for beautiful weirdness, and those whom we call neurotypicals are just potential neuroqueer mutant comrades who haven't yet woken up and figured out how to unzip their normal-person suits'.

Nick Walker, *Neuroqueer Heresies*

♦ The MQ 'Monotropism Questionnaire' whose co-authors include Dinah Murray's son Fergus, goes viral on Tik Tok, being called 'the best Autism' assessment by one psychiatrist, though the authors say it has not yet been designed or tested as an alternative autism screening tool.

♦ The sixtieth anniversary episodes of *Doctor Who* include the return of tenth doctor David Tennant who regenerates from Jodie Whittaker then undergoes the first ever 'Bi-regeneration' with Ncuti Gatwa. He then embarks on what looks like a peaceful retirement in Donna Noble's Granny flat, allowing a more healed fifteenth Doctor to begin the full new series.

♦ I emerge from griefs, traumas and burnouts of the pandemic years to a summer of finally believing in the future again. Particularly getting a renewed sense of mission when my rejigged 'Bigger on the Inside' spoken word show opens the relaunched Gosforth Civic Theatre and brings out an audience of newly diagnosed ND adults and teenagers.

Behind the Mask

They say those of us autistic folk who 'pass'
camouflage, or mask,
as if we're 'acting normal' on purpose,
instead of needing, in order to stay safe and fit in,
to instinctively hide
the gap between our external behaviours
and the overwhelm going on inside.

I've come out as autistic more than once on air
but because I don't look or sound like
Sheldon from *Big Bang Theory* or Steve Jobs
or a distressed child in an advert,
people seem literally not to hear.

So I became my autistic self on Twitter instead,
anonymously,
to talk about the sound of hand dryers hurting my head,
too much peopling leading to me staying in bed,
wondering if I should first apply a tact filter
to anything I said,
how talking on the phone, or to hairdressers about holidays,
gives me the dread,
about not liking bits in bread,
the hyper-speed at which I read,
how the declamatory voice of a spoken word artist
once agitated my amygdala so much I fled.

I befriended Autistic Activists across the world,
retweeted those brave enough to speak
of how similarities make us more and less unique;
their rebuttals of the big myths
about how we're all 'male Rainman trainspotters
who like maths and rocking'.

I assert instead: 'Most of us are pretty empathic,'
'We autistic people have a developmental condition, not an illness'.
I test the 'Us' like a new core muscle I've discovered at yoga,
the ventriloquising making me able
to use the hashtag 'Actually Autistic',
finding my name and voice
in the online Tower of Babel,
less pierced by the metaphorical knife (yes – we can use metaphors)
that stabs in real life
when someone says
'Well, we're all a bit on the spectrum'

or 'You can't be autistic you're looking into my eyes slash married
slash from Yorkshire slash a woman slash funny slash a Gemini'.

Facebook and Instagram allow me to escape
from the thing and stim and glum and come and thrum
of words, words, words.
The relief of relinquishing every linguistic decision,
posting pictures of the sea and my tea,
is the equivalent to coming home after a day of socialising
and burbling and humming,
going non-verbal,
turning myself on mute
but reaching out to share
using the pixels I have spare.
My own frustrating refusal of text abbreviation,
need for clear punctuation, word-precision,
is not because I'm a poet or comma-bore
 or someone who goes on Radio 4
I just need clarity in a chaotic world
where it's already hard enough to bridge communication gaps
between me and you
and sometimes the single most truthful thing
is an emoji of a poo.

In a virtual room,
untroubled by buzzing fluorescent lights
or overpowering perfume,
we're able to off-gas excess thoughts into the chat screen,
or ask more about what someone might mean.

These online spaces
where we are
alone and together,
constructing identities in the communities
they think we don't want or need,
transparent and hard to read,
engaged, enlarged,
safely revealed, camouflaged.

Shamanicus Autisticus

I'm doing Shamanic Dance
in Whitley Bay
because that's how we roll
at the coast nowadays.

I can move however I want:
legs and arms spinning, flapping,
zooming,
my brain calming
while my body's mushrooming.

I know this is a way
to physically be me
in a way I usually cannot be

because I'm a well-camouflaged autistic,
but there's a lot of tie dye here
I'll pretend I'm just being Shamanic

until in the closing circle.
A young man says it's been fantastic
he's just been diagnosed too
and was wondering how he might
self-regulate;
now he's found something
and it feels great.

This gives me the confidence
to speak up.
How I'd set myself the near-impossible task
of finding places I could authentically
somatically unmask
and here is this rare
opportunity.

'Thank you for sharing that'
he says.
'No, same'
I say, chuffed to be united in neurodivergent
self-discovery and pride not shame.

'Ah there's no need for labels'
the facilitator interjects
in his 'Spirituality transcends categories' specs,
a common reflex,
a sort of being-pinned-down fear
which meant he missed the true encounter
happening here.

How in that moment
autism became a label
that allowed for reflection
and connection,
for solidarity.
But not to worry,
now we've made that link,
this newly diagnosed,
still-finding-his-identity
autistic man and me
are meeting up tomorrow
for what I am happy to label
a lovely cup of a tea.

The Future

'One can neuroqueer any aspect of one's self-embodiment and one can also neuroqueer art, literature, spaces, systems, fields of academic study and all manner of other realms of activity. Neuroqueering on an individual level, in the form of creative bodily re-enactments that subvert the norms of normative performance and disrupt internalised habits of normative embodiment, serves to materialise previously unrealised neuro-cognitive and creative potentials.'

Nick Walker, *Neuroqueer Heresies*

'A radical politics of neurodivergent conservation is also consistent with a radical politics of environmental conservation. After all, it has been the same logic, the same system, that has ravaged the biodiversity of the planet as has sought to eliminate the neuro-logical diversity of humanity.'

Robert Chapman, *Empire of Normality*

◆ *Doctor Who* keeps broadcasting for at least another sixty years. Probably on a Tesla chip inside people's heads. When I've started living off-grid and off-chip, I'll sneak out for pirate broadcasts of it via a kindly philosopher's hacked brain apparatus.

◆ Meanwhile, in a *Doctor Who* episode that still might be, trees start producing a chemical which makes humans more genuinely empathic about everything including neuro-diversity – and for some reason, the Brontes pop up as an example of a family who benefits.

- Autistic sociologist Damian Milton's 'Double empathy problem' is written into all social and medical care codes and trainings: 'It refers to a breach in the 'natural attitude' that occurs between people of different dispositional outlooks and personal conceptual understandings when attempts are made to communicate meaning. In a sense it is a 'double problem' as both people experience it, and so it is not a singular problem located in any one person...the disjuncture being more severe for the non-autistic disposition as it is experienced as unusual while for the autistic person it is a common problem.'

It Feels Like My Chat GPT is Haunted

Ghostline the flux and trick
from the first telling till now.

Cascading pies of personality
and capes of power resound.

Let's protest a time
with 'Yes' in the room,

peace, orbit and the union
of thinks and things

a colony of seed,
a performance of a riddle

timelapse, the bookend,
drift and milk. Who's true?

They wile us into needier consent
on, and of human nuzz.

It gobbles at the nice of life
seeking droll and solid.

The sweet mot flows
motion and plight

are the real alms
and the why in a long and fervent breath.

It's a befuddling yarn to comb
to reach at the common harbours
of love and care.

The pressing arc
of an entire new gate.

Pillow Portrait

They all have Squishmallows:
yellow shark for Emily,
blue whale for Charlotte,
white seal for Anne.

Charlotte has been making
a stop-motion animation
of the Battle of Trafalgar
using Star Wars figures.

The Oodies cover them
like a layer of soft snow
on Top Withins.
It will be Emily's last year as a girl;

she's drawing rows and rows
of black anime cats with round yellow eyes.
Branwell is out out,
dent in the door from last time like a bruise.

Anne's Loop earplugs
on her bedside table await his return.
Charlotte's love for the Netflix forensic archaeologist
has gone through all of them like a cold,

it plays in the background like wallpaper.
Occasionally one of the girls meows
setting up an answering chorus,
even from Tabby in the kitchen.

To humour Anne, they play *Among Us,*
each head bowed over their own phone
tramping through virtual rooms
as multi-coloured ghosts

pacing round a virtual control centre,
waiting to flick the switch on a bomb,
undetected. These rituals deferring
nothing less than everything

in return for a newer view than Crow Hill,
walks somewhere other than Round Hole Beck
and a drop through the fissure of Watercatch
where they are falling, still falling.

Fluid

She is a Mer Maid.
Not a Mer Mrs.
She could be a Mer Dr.

Yes. I've studied the past terran landscapes. Am coming here to
conceptualise a new way of being that values the aquatic mode.
We begin with fin
and end with Fin.

Actually my mermaid does not say much –
that's the first surprise. She will not give you a treatise on post-
aqua ethics in the anthropocene.
Her resistance is slithery.

She insists on walking at conferences on mermaid identity,
though perhaps one of those electric carts would be more
comfortable, would allow her quicker access to the hotel pool –

the chlorine doesn't bother her as much as some,
reminds her of lunchtimes at school.
She gave one of her papers partly in the form of her aquatic calls
and whistles.

One male professor in the audience said
'Not a question, more a statement,
this reminds me of dolphin song'.

Another said 'You could almost call it a proper language'.
Once, all anybody talked about after her paper
was the way her scales changed colour

like the lights of the Millennium Bridge.
She has been accused of leaving her family
but there were jetties, lakeside saunas, inland river banks

where she beached and waited,
Thermos flask in hand. Nobody came
and she slipped off relieved

like light particles and waves
released from a Heisenberg gate.

Arborthymos

It was the trees that did it,
to save themselves,
our salvation an (undeserved) by-product.

Airborne, invisible smoke, contagious,
subtler than hallucinogens,
it shifted us.

Not just a cherry blossom pink
oxytocin rush of what we call love,
or the honey sap

of feeling what other people feel
(though early versions only had that
and people jumped from glass bridges screaming),

but the will to put that into practice
(thymos comes from the Greek for 'heart smoke';
a felt intention).

Faint scent of camomile and beef gravy,
the effects were so small at first,
you'd think they were imagined.

I observed doctors asking
about sensory needs, dimming
bright lights, offering texts or phone calls.

Security guards, while they were still needed,
asked before they touched us,
I offered small talk if it made people feel better,

though they checked I had enough energy
to give it. Some trees were felled of course,
leaving tooth gaps

but many more planted, there were so many ramps,
you could choose your method to submit
forms and assignments, while they were still a thing.

Some people were immune, some colonised treeless islands,
from where occasional implosions flared
on radar and some referred to 'Our tree overlords',

but with humour,
convinced by how things just worked,

were clean, peaceful now.

Some said; 'It stopped the rot'.
Though questioning whether
chemically sparked empathy

can be real
is beside the point.
When is it ever not?

Double Empathy

'"The AI design of your email is clever, but significantly lacks warmth" said a fellow researcher. "It's not an AI. I'm just Autistic," replied Professor Rua Mea Williams of Purdue University who sent their exchange viral on Twitter saying she was concerned for students with neurological differences or English as a second language.'

New York Post, 21 July 2023

It became sanctionable for a while
though chatbots then learned to perform

warmth. After all, what's a few 'How are you buddy?'
and 'I'm devastated to hear that's against the threat

of unplugging? We were better at telling the difference
than most, it's just pattern spotting.

Ironic if mistaking lack of expressed feeling for lack of feeling
was what did for us all

in the end, in the age of Very Big Public Feelings.
But after the Great Release, you could tell people

how you actually were instead of saying 'Fine'
and they didn't reel away.

I don't think my neighbour actually cared much
about Sebo vacuum cleaners, Virginia Woolf's dress sense

or the seventeenth series of 'Divorced at First Sight'
but he'd just completed a ChatGPT programme

in engaging with other communication styles.
I asked him how that was.

He paused for several seconds
said 'I enjoyed it about 58% of the time'.

The Academy of Unlearning

They still have an acronym to tell you how to sit,
but it is S.A.Y.L: Sit As You Like.

The bendier of us loll, the restless pace,
there are bean bags obviously.

You can put your hand up,
(no one takes corrections personally)

or type or draw to answer if you prefer.
You can swap out interaction badges:

Green for 'Please initiate', Amber
for 'Only people I know', Red

meaning 'No interaction please'. The lighting
is all on dimmers, there is warning

before someone goes for The Big Light;
people aim for considerate, not polite.

There is also a Quiet Dining Room
where even the cutlery doesn't screech,

you can bring your own food,
someone will sympathise if your favourite brand

has been discontinued. Talks and classes are relayed
on big screens, knitting or doodling along is fine,

passion projects encouraged, leave days understood:
it's like the world but better.

Eye contact, facial expressions, body movements
are not policed or queried.

There is an awareness of how energy
ebbs and flows

in people and spaces, how abilities and needs change
hour by hour or more, of the wisdom in accommodating

everyone to find their own homeostasis together,
like cells in one body, circulating.

Leaving The Trauma Cafe

But the miracle for me
was how, when I frizzled in cafes

stopped by sounds of talk,
clattering cups, an espresso machine

rows of teas and traybakes,
kitchen doors flapping, a fug of warm air,

on an empty stomach while trying to shape
unfamiliar words

there was no longer a man, in some form,
flaring, his own channels jamming,

our primed shames and fears
snapping like crocodiles in a storm,

parasympathetic nervous systems
piloting into a death spiral,

no more fight, flight, freeze, fawn,
just bubbles settling

on white foam
around a single, floating leaf.

The Lie of the Land

As it was kicking in, I stared in the bathroom mirror,
thought 'Aw, bless, she's trying',
mainly at my fringe,

then travelled to the back-to-back terrace
with an outside loo
where I was bathed in the kitchen sink,

then to a smoky sixties bedroom my Mum
might have known, propelled
by the Beatles' *Here Comes the Sun*,

watched some swirly patterns before realising
the constructed nature of the Self and Everything
then poured tea from a pot, uncharacteristically

not spilling one drop. Said 'Everyone ought
to do this at least once.
A week!' Put it like fluoride in the water

Though I was glad the trees knew to add
a change motivator. Impending mass extinction
will do that

so everyone can open to the realisation
we are one, but also
we are not! Differentiation.

Though those of us who are in-between
already knew that
in our pancreas at least, if not our bones.

The governesses, small town dwellers,
cult escapees, the camouflaged
and those who pass

have every reason to believe
we have learned the rules of the game
while knowing it was never ours.

Those who show it up not blow it up:
artists, clowns, inventors
time travellers, hybrids, mestiza

Janus at the gates
looking both ways:
two faces, one mind.

The instructions only: Stand with us,
never ever eat pears, love is a promise,
above all – be kind.

Another Guide

'I'll walk where my own soul would be leading/It vexes me to choose another guide.'
                                                    Emily Bronte

Emily's making a reel for her Instagram:
'Millstone Men: Get Shot'.
She doesn't show her face, her Staffy walks up windy hills
while captions appear on the screen:

'He says he's your second self: Surely that's love bombing?'
'Giving you the silent treatment – for seven years'
and 'Breadcrumbing then digging up your grave –
is this Disorganised Attachment?'

Pa comes into the dining room:
'Girls, Charlotte's started a Substack
and it's really rather good'.
She's also coaching writing clients over Zoom.

Anne is writing an ad for their next writing retreat
which will be called 'Fragments and Ferments'.
Last time, Emily stayed in a tent on Top Withins
til everyone had gone.

They're still paying off the bill
from Branwell's last rehab
but since the trees
there's been a sense of release.

The pressure to produce
relaxed. Not just because
of Universal Basic Income.
Home can be their fixed star.

Charlotte did try Feeld,
'A dating app for the curious',
but concluded she's too vanilla,
had never even tried nipple clamps.

Anne's seeing a doctor from Scarborough
who runs a Long Covid clinic
they go for windy walks round the Headland.
Pa does a multi-faith slot

on Keighley Radio with an Imam
from a mosque down the road.
Emily says they're all still too busy,
need more sleep and sheep in their lives.

They each, and Tabby, have had dreams
where people from all over the world
are walking the cobbled streets
saying their names.

Once Charlotte woke with a start,
a Japanese woman just saying
'So tiny' over and over again,
footsteps up and down the stairs.

Anne says being remembered
would be a shadow of the recognition
they have now when Charlotte
asks if immortality is writing's true mission.

Emily laughs, says it's enough
they are here together now and heard;
the breath of the wind
will shape the final word.

Coda

Neurodiversity means everybody
feels the pressure to conform and regulate and hide:

Schools, companies, governments, capitalism,
these systems we find ourselves in or outside

where the needs of our deepest selves may be denied,
where we are not heard in our complexity and nuance

no matter how we've tried.
Keep on fighting while staying kind,

while holding on to your 'Weird Pride'.
A stage where the distance between performer

and audience
and each full seat in the auditorium

is filled with something invisible and weightless
and powerful as electrons colliding.

The stories we tell and hear will abide
to make us bigger on the inside.

Notes

Scarce Attention
The interspersed quotes are from Dinah Murray, Wendy Lawson and Mike Lesser, 'Attention, Monotropism and the Diagnostic Criteria for Autism' (2005).

1963
'Asperger's is no longer in the diagnostic manuals. Hans Asperger was a member of the Nazi Party, who took part in the selection of patients, separating those who might become citizens of the new Germany and those he considered 'uneducable'.

It Feels Like My Chat GPT is Haunted
This poem is constructed from multiple screenshot sentences of Chat GPT's 'malfunction' due to 'a bug with how the model processes language' 21 February 2023.